WHEN FATHERS DON'T HUG

JAMES KIRKWOOD

Published in the United States of America

Brilliant Books Literary
137 Forest Park Lane Thomasville
North Carolina 27360 USA

CONTENTS

ACKNOWLEDGMENTS

I would like to thank my children for putting up with me all these years, take the good and bad from me and try and do a better job with your kids. To my cousins, James and Carl Young, thanks for being there for me. To Pastor Ralph D. West, thank you for the confirmation. Last but not least I wish to avail myself this opportunity to Thank God for keeping me around and express a sense gratitude and love to my friends and my beloved parents for their support, strength, help and everything else.

FOREWORD

If you have a father that does not hug or a father that did not hug, I writing this book in hope that you can reflect on my relationship/experiences with my father and realize that your father does/did care and loves/loved you, even if you did not get any hugs. Each chapter in this book is an experience that I had with my father. I hope this book will help you look at your pass relationships/ experiences with your father and if he is still living, start, rekindle a relationship with him and if he has passed, find that one experience that you can hold on to that lets you know that your father did care and loved you.

After I wrote my first draft of this book, I sent a copy to my cousin, Carl Young. He has is a gifted, I mean gifted speaker and author. He spent a lot of time with our uncle, Rev. James (Uncle Bubba) Smith. I think a lot of Uncle Bubba rubbed off on Carl. He recommended that I include some lessons learned after each chapter. I thought about it and decided that I would include them. Then I started really thinking about those experiences, and what would be some lessons learned. I think lessons learned are not where I want you to go; I want you to really think about the same or similar type experiences with your father. So I included what I am calling "Reflective". Reflective by definition is "relating to or characterized by deep thought", that is what I would like you to focus on.

I think it is important for you to understand where my head was when I was growing up. We are all a factor of our environment, that's no debate. Like my long time elementary, junior high and high school classmate, Larry "Buzzard" Johnson says. "We did not know we were poor until they told us we were. We had food to eat, clothes to wear, and a place to stay, everything was good from our viewpoint". The only thing I had to compare my childhood to was the other kids in the neighborhood. And from that standpoint, I was doing well. I did not have to share a room with a brother and I had a way of making some money.

One thing that stuck in my head from all that time Mama made me go to church was, Honor thou mother and father, for thou days will be long. So I did 95% of what they said. I made sure I did not get caught doing that 5%. I just thought that all of those things I did growing up were things I was suppose to do. I never gave it any thought. Well let's get started.

It was during marriage counseling with my second wife, third marriage that gave me the idea for this book. I married my first wife twice. During one of the sessions, the counselor started asking about my mother and father, but more so about my father. The questions centered around, did he have a temper? What kind of relationship did we have? Did I receive hugs from him? And was he a mean person? The counselor and my now ex wife (who has a Masters Degree in Social Work) concluded that I was deficient in the caring area because of the answers I gave to the questions. Well things went south from that point on during the counseling session. I could have saved those seventy-five dollars. I understand that each one of us is a product of our mother and father and who knows how far back in the generations a person goes to pick up traits. Oh, the answers I gave to the questions were: Yes, Great, None, some people say "Yes", (he was never mean to me, but I did on occasions see him get very upset with people). They really freaked out when I said my father never hugged me. The main reason I disagreed with them was, although

I have a lot of my father's traits, I hugged both my son and daughter while they were growing up and still do to this day. I guess I got that from my mother, although she did not hug me until she was late in her years. She lived to be 96. But that is another book.

All of this got me to thinking. Did my father love me? Did he really care? Well let's see what the smart folks have to say about it.

The simple act of a hug isn't just felt on our arms. When we embrace someone, oxytocin (also known as "the cuddle hormone") is released, making us feel all warm and fuzzy inside. The chemical has also been linked to social bonding. "Oxytocin is a neuropeptide, which basically promotes feelings of devotion, trust and bonding," DePauw University psychologist Matt Hertenstein stated. "It really lays the biological foundation and structure for connecting to other people." Researchers have long suspected that biological responses to stress may be shaped early in life. Now, in the experiment with rats, researchers at Emory University in Atlanta and McGill University in Montreal say they have confirmed a connection between touch and stress.

"High-quality maternal-infant interaction -- lots of time spent grooming, licking, nursing in the rats -- correlated with animals that were quite capable of dealing with stress as adults," said Paul Plotsky, of Emory University. "Those offspring ... of mothers who spent less time in maternal behavior toward them were hyper-reactive to stress."

Researchers also compared the brain chemistry of the two groups of rats, looking specifically for levels of hormones released during times of stress. They found that as adults, rats that had been cuddled had significantly reduced levels of those hormones. The researchers believe the results show that development of babies is controlled by more than genetics -- that it's both nature and nurture.

And even before they had the chance to test their theory in humans, the researchers said there's enough evidence of a possible link to support plenty of baby hugs.

Well, I did not get any hugs growing up, but I serviced twenty-nine years in the U.S. Army and retired as a Colonel, if that is not dealing with stress, I do not know what is. And that is all I have to say about that.

Introduction

If you did not read the Forward, do yourself a favor and go back and read it. The rest of this book will make more sense. Go ahead, it will not take long.

Now you will be able to relate to what I am saying. I guess the best way to start is to tell you about my father. His name was Everett Kirkwood. He was born on November 27, 1901, 3 miles southeast of Colmesneil, Texas. Colmesneil is approximately sixty four miles north of Beaumont, Texas. He was the oldest son of Rev. Ernest and Clara Kirkwood. Son, as he was called by members of the family, worked on the family farm and attended school in Colmesneil. He loved to hunt and fish, which help put food on the table. When he was fifteen years old, his father was killed and he had to drop out of school to help support his mother, brother and sisters.

(Everett Kirkwood)

Let me divert and tell you about his parents and grand-parents, it will shed a little light of Everett's childhood development.

On his father's side:

His father, Rev. Ernest Kirkwood, was born August 17, 1879, the offspring of Sarah Ann McCullough F.G.C. (Free Woman of Color), born May 10, 1837 in Mississippi. It was told to me that she had three children by Lars Sandlin, a Swedish slave owner. Sarah Ann later married George W. Kirkwood F.M.C. (Free Man of Color) in Comanche, Texas in 1886.

("Free man of color, F.M.C." and "free woman of color, F.G.C. " were legal terms used to describe non-slaves in the Southern United States. It distinguished them from their white counterparts, who often had the same name.)

(Ernest Kirkwood)

It is said that he killed himself. However, it was told to me that he was killed by a white man that was seeing his

wife's sister and was killed so that he would not say anything. I have the shotgun that he supposedly used and it is no way you can pull the trigger with your toe and shoot yourself in the head. Plus, he was found with his shoes on. And that is all I have to say about that.

On his mother's side:

On January 12, 1898, Ernest married Clara C. Simpson, who was born July 7, 1879 in Colmesneil, Texas to James Charles Simpson F.M.C., born December 1844 in Alexandria, Louisiana and Margarett Gilder F.G.C., born June, 1844 in Macon Georgia.

(Clara Simpson Kirkwood)

WHEN FATHERS DON'T HUG

(Jim & Margarett Simpson)

His grandfather, James "Jim" Charles was purchased by the Clark family and given the Clark sir name until he and his brother decided to change it. Jim, as he was known, told his descendants that he and his brother Charlie remembered taking food cooked by his mother to their real father, James Simpson, at the machine shop which he owned. James Simpson was an Irish landowner who settled in Alexandria, Louisiana. Jim occasionally worked in the shop with his father. The boys called him "Mr. Simpson". Jim had a half brother, Frank Simpson, who was bold, brazen, and demanding. He was a young whippersnapper with the true White Syndrome who insisted that plantation hands call him "Mr. Frank". Jim Clark, knowing that Frank was his half brother, refused to call him "Mr. Frank".

One day Frank told Jim he was going into town to buy a new whip so he could whip his ass the next time he (Jim) refused to call him "Mr. Frank". Frank returned from town on horseback and found Jim chopping 'commodities' (clearing the weeds out of the garden). Jim called him Frank and Frank started hitting Jim with his whip. The whip wrapped around Jim but left the hand holding the hoe free. He raised the hoe and struck Frank on the head. Frank died as a result of the blow.

Following the incident, Jim immediately took his younger brother, Charlie, and escape through the swamps and woodlands of southern Louisiana until they reached the river. They crossed the river and stepped on Texas soil. The two brothers felt they would be Free in Texas and hence Jim would not be punished for killing his half-brother in Louisiana. After the river crossing, Jim and Charlie agreed they would take their Father's sir name and would never allow anyone to call them Clark again. Hence, they became James "Jim" Simpson and Charles "Charlie" Calvin Simpson. Although both were good hunters and fishermen, times were hard. Jim sent Charlie back across the river (Louisiana border) where life would be easier for the younger brother. Jim told him to tell everyone that: "I made you leave to keep you from telling on me but you had escaped to return home". The brothers never meet again.

Jim remained in Texas to make a life for himself. He kept on the move until 1867 when he arrived in Tyler County, Texas. Jim agreed to sharecrop a tract of land over a period of several years but at the end of one year with his figuring skills he purchased the land from the holder of the lease and became a land owner on December 19, 1879 (90 acres, still in the family). He was respected for his opinions and was sought after by numerous men. After becoming a landowner, he even sat on the jury in Tyler County. Jim was well known for his word and often stated: "My word is my bond". He lived by that statement and it was his personal code. Jim was not much on 'Going to Church' but preferred to live his Christianity day by day. He died in 1925 and is buried in the Mt. Zion Cemetery Colmesneil, Texas.

Jim Simpson married Margarett Gilder F.G.C. in 1868. Margarett Gilder F.G.C. told her children and grandchildren how she and her family, along with other slaves, had walked from Macon, Georgia to Colmesneil, Texas. She had thirteen children, however only nine are recorded. She died from a bout with small pox contracted while visiting in Beaumont, Texas in 1918 and is buried at the Mt. Zion Cemetery Colmesneil, Texas.

Let's get back to Everett. After his father was killed, Everett worked at the Saw Mill and on the Railroad. He was also known to have blended a good batch of "moon shine", which he stored above his mother's kitchen. There was not much to do after work and playing baseball was the order of the afternoon. Everett could run fast and throw hard. He played outfield because of his speed and pitched because of his arm. Pitching is where he excelled. Everett developed the ability to throw a fast ball, a curve ball and a knuckle ball. What made him effective was his ability to throw these three pitches over hand, three-quarter and side arm, which gave him nine pitches. Everett played for the Houston Black Buffalos, in the Southern League which was one of the 56 leagues that made up the Negro League. He also played in Mexico until he broke his leg. His best moment was when he pitched and won the final game in the 1921 Little Negro World Series, where the Houston Black Buffalos beat the White House of David in Austin, Texas. The winning ball and a plaque are in the Negro Leagues Baseball Museum in Kansas City, MO.

(Everett Kirkwood – Pitcher Houston Black Buffalos)

Everett and his four cousins learned to barbeque from his Uncle, Charlie Simpson. All five went into the barbeque business. During World War II, Everett served with the Combat Engineers as a cook, increasing his culinary skills and his ability to blow up stuff. Upon release from the Army, he returned to Austin. Relying on his skills, he opened a "barbeque pit" now call a restaurant. He later moved to Houston and opened Kirkwood's Barbeque, which he operated for over 30 years. In addition, "Kirk", as he was known by his clients and customers, also contracted as a hunting guide/tracker and cook for over thirty years on deer, elk, and bear hunts as well as fishing expeditions. He also catered parties for such notables as Lyndon Baines Johnson and other Texas state and local politicians. Daddy never went to church, but read the bible every night. He was much like his grandfather Jim Simpson, in that he tried to live his Christianity.

As I mentioned above, my dad was born November 27, 1901 and my mother was born February 12, 1914. I was born June 1, 1950, you do the math. When I was growing up, I thought there were only people my age and old folks. We were never around any people in their thirties or forties. I was born to old parents. Not only in years, also in old fashion ideals. I came up where children were seen and not heard and where a firm handshake had meaning.

Daddy only whipped me three times in his life. I am calling them whippings; his method was to have you lay on your stomach with your hands under you. As he whipped you, he told you not to move, impossible. Those three whippings were because I did not do what he told me to do. About three weeks after the last whipping, I went to him and said. "Daddy, I am not trying to be funny, but I hope you enjoyed that last whipping you gave me because that was the last time. I got it, when you say do something, do it then or do it by a certain time. But, do it."

Reflective:

I knew the story of my grandfather and did not understand what had happen back then and how it affected my father until I was in my teens and the Civil Rights movement was going on. I just learned the story of my great grandparents approximately eight years ago. You would think Daddy would have deep resentment of white people, but he did not. However he said "Do not trust policemen and politicians, because they are both crooked than a barrel of snakes and keep people at arm's length, black or whatever color, until you know where they are coming from". Homework:

Try and find out as much as you can about your father's childhood, his parents and grandparents. Some of the struggles they had could shed some light on why your father acts/acted the way he does and what his values are/were. Do not be so quick to judge.

LEARNING TO WORK

I had to work at the "barbeque pit" on Saturdays. I do not remember how old I was when I started; it was before I was playing little league baseball. Baseball was the only thing that got me out of working at the "barbeque pit". I do remember having to stack three empty soda water (you all call it soda pop or pop) crates on top of each other to be tall enough to reach down in the sink to wash dishes. My job duties were to wait on customers, wash dishes, chop and bust wood (will explain this one later), turn meat, sweep up and mop, help make sausages, help cut up a fourth on a cow and season it to be cooked and whatever else it was to do. At first I did not want to work every Saturday, I wanted to play with my friends. Daddy always told me to learn how to barbeque, if I could not make a living with my education, I could always fall back on barbequing. No one could take that from me. (Caring)

Daddy did not believe in the child labor law back then, according to my first cousin, James Young, who stayed with my parents during the summers when he was a teenager and worked at the "barbeque pit". I do not believe there were child labor laws then. James had the same job duties as I did.

The "barbeque pit" was not that big. There was a counter with fifteen stools to serve customers and a table in the corner that seated four. Behind the counter was a long ice box that we put real ice in to keep the soda water (soda or pop) cold. He did not sell beer because a lot of church folks were customers and plus he did not want the hassle of dealing with drunks. He did let customers go next door to the beer joint and bring a beer in to drink with their meal. The cutting block and the actual pit itself were visible to the customers, so they could see the preparation of the food. There was no air condition, just an exhaust fan that took the smoke out. On one wall, there was this big picture frame, about five feet by four feet, which contain pictures of all the hunts he had been on and above it was a fourteen point deer that he killed; it was the largest rack deer he ever killed.

A typical Saturday morning started at 6:00 am, with a "get out of the bed so we can go". The first stop was the meat packing company, where he purchased a fourth of a cow (four quarter) and boxes of frozen Polk ribs. Sometimes we had to stop at the seasoning company to buy ingredients to make his seasoning to go on the meat. Once we got to the "barbeque pit", he started the fire in the fire box, put the meat he had already cooked on the pit to get hot and started to cut up and trim the four quarter. Once we got the big pieces of meat and ribs seasoned and put on the pit, we then had to make sausages with the trimmings from the four quarter. When I say make sausages, I mean make sausages. He bought hog guts (casings), washed them, cut them in the specific length and tired one end with a string. There was this big red electric meat grinder that we used to grind up the meat that sit on this long counter in the "back" along with the hand crank sausage stuffer. In the "back" was a long counter attached to the wall, the fire box for the pit, a refrigerator where the potatoe salad was kept and a three compartment sink to wash dishes. The sink consisted of one sink to wash the dishes, one with a gas burner under it to keep it at 180 degrees to dip the dishes in. We stuffed about two hundred sausages every Saturday. The next thing I had to do was clean up the front (sweep and mop) and get ready for the lunch crowd. All of this was done before 11:00 am.

When the lunch crowd came in, I had to wait on the people sitting at the counter and the table and take to go orders. Once the lunch rush was over, it was time to wash the dishes and sweep up the front area. Remember me saying that the fire box and the sink with the burner under it were in the "back". It was hot back there during the summer, I mean hot. It was hotter than fish grease. It was great in the winter. During the summer months, you could wash dishes and come out to the front and it felt like there was an air conditioner running.

Daddy only bought a small amount of split wood. If someone had cut down an oak, hickory or pecan tree, he would have the big pieces delivered and put behind the "barbeque pit" where the wood was stacked to dry out. It was my job to split up the large pieces and chop them into fire wood size. I used a double blade ax, a 16 pound slug hammer and two iron wedges. Let's just say that I had the biggest arms of any kid my age. That splitting and chopping wood paid off when I played little league baseball. After swinging that 16 pound slug hammer, that ax felt like a tooth pick.

The "barbeque pit" was located about three miles from downtown Houston in a White and Hispanic area. When all of the work was completed, I could go down the street and play with David and Tommy (Hispanic brothers). That is how I learned to speak Spanish. Sometime I went to the movies at the Jenson Drive picture show (theater). It was one of two picture shows a black person could go to in Houston that you did not have to sit in the balcony.

Daddy did believe in paying you. After he would cut the meat off the bone, he would sell the bone with some meat on it as what he called "regulars". The meat is sweetness next to the bone. Folks would come in and order "regulars" which was a two pound brown bag filled with bones, some barbeque sauce poured over them with two slices of bread for fifty cent. No matter what the "regulars" sells were, I got all of it. That could be ten dollars or as much as thirty dollars, it just depended on sells. Not bad money for a kid back then.

Oh, I also had to cut the yard at home. Daddy cut the grass one time. He had so many zigzags in it, Mama told him not to cut it anymore. I think he did that on purpose so I would end up cutting the grass. I did not get paid for cutting the grass.

Remember I said, Daddy cooked on deer hunts and catered barbeque banquets. During my last year in high school, Daddy closed up the barbeque pit and worked for J.H. Rose Truck line, specifically for Mr. Ebb Rose, VP, cooking for banquets and preparing for all the hunts they went on. I remember one summer, the Liberty River over flowed and flooded Mr. Ebb's ranch in Dayton, Texas. This left the livestock on the ranch stranded in the high water and the pastures were not fit for grazing. So I and some other hands had to get on horseback and pull the livestock out of the water to dry land. Since the pasture land was destroyed at that ranch, he moved the livestock to his Huntsville, Texas ranch. With the additional livestock at the Huntsville ranch, the pasture land would not support the combination of both ranches.

The result was an auction and barbeque. Mr. Ebb had four cows processed and purchased one hundred chickens for the event. The actual pit was at least 20 feet long and five feet wide. The beef did not have to be turned that much, but those chickens were work. As soon as you had turned all of them, you had to start all over again. We also had to prepare potatoe salad, hush puppies, slice onions and beans for the five hundred expected guests. Daddy was in his late sixties then, so I had to do most of the work. Because it was a big party to cater, Daddy hired two other people to help with the preparation and four servers. Of course, my Mother was there to supervise the potatoe salad preparation. I ended up supervising all of them, except Mama. While I was wiping sweat after turning the meat and chickens, I saw Daddy, Mama and Mr. Ebb standing over where we were boiling the potatoes talking. Later, Mama can over and told me that Mr. Ebb gave me several complements on my work ethics and how I had taken charge and everything was running smooth. Daddy never said anything to me about it, but as I remember observing them while they were talking, I saw that smile come over his face. I call it his approval/proud smile.

Reflective:

When I was growing up, the only professional black folks were Teachers, Preachers, a few Doctors, Policemen, Politicians and Lawyers. Like I said, the Civil Rights movement was going on and the future for black folks, was to me, up in the air. At that early age, I was not thinking about a career. I learned the value of a dollar, how to manage my money, ways to make money, how to operate a business, and how to treat people. Think back, there has to be some time in your life when your Father told you something or there are something that he did that you still follow or do today.

LEARNING TO SURVIVE

As far back as I can remember Daddy, Mama and I would go to Colmesneil, Texas (the old home place) to fish, hunt and put in a garden. It was more than a garden; we grew corn, watermelons, peas, sugar cane and some other items, cannot remember the other items. Guess who had to hoe out the weeds. We also made sugar cane syrup which they sold. I did not like the beer that came off of the process. You also had to watch out for that piece of timber that was attach to the press and to the tractor as you feed stacks of cane between these rollers. Daddy built what he called "the camp". The camp was a tin building approximately 600 sq feet, with a fire place in the middle made out of the steel molds used to make blocks of ice which had a 55 gallon drum on the roof filled with used oil. A tube ran from the drum down to the fire box which had an on /off valve. You could burn wood in the fire place and the oil was used to start the fire or keep it going. It also had an L-shape screen in porch that included the kitchen and room to sleep if it was too hot inside. He did have electricity run to it, so we had lights. The kitchen consisted of an old ice box, an old electric refrigerator and a stove that was made out of the same molds used to make the fire place. It even had an oven. On the other hand, my daddy's his first cousin, Tom Forward, built a three bedroom house on the land with two sleeping porches and a huge den. He stayed up there more than we did. He had done well in the BBQ business in Dallas, Texas.

The place was perfect for learning to shoot and track game, learning what you could eat and what not to eat in the woods and how to find it, fishing (with a pole and without a pole), hunting with and without a gun, building a shelter and just having the freedom of 90 acres all to myself. My first gun was a BB gun. I did a lot of shooting at card broad targets in the back yard. Daddy gave me his Springfield single shot 22 rifle when I was nine years old; this was a year before my mother knew I was shooting a real gun and she thought I was too young then.

From about eight years old until I was twelve, Daddy and cousin Tom would teach me the skills they had learned from those old folks in the family. Cousin Tom did not have any children although he had been married several times and Daddy and he were like brothers, so they both taught me.

Skills I had to master:

Rubber Boots:

This is not a skill, but Daddy insisted that I wear these knee high rubber boots when I left the camp house. He said "Snakes cannot bite through them, just in case you do not see the snake." (Caring) He had been bitten by a rattlesnake on the foot walking barefoot when he was a kid.

Shooting:

The 22 was easy to shoot. I had shot that BB gun so much it was not that much difference. The 22 did not have a scope, but it did have a white material on the front sight that if a light was put on it, you could aim in the dark. Great for hunting Raccoons and Ring tails at night. Daddy always told me not to load the rifle unless I was going to shoot something. Me being the logical person that I am, I thought that I could put a round in the chamber, as long as I did not cock the hammer. Well, I was playing soldier one day at the camp, practicing movement with the rifle. When I brought the weapon down, the butt hit the ground and the rifle fired, the bullet just missed my head. I could hear him say, "Hard head brings a soft butt". (Caring)

Tracking game:

There were deer, wild turkey, squirrels, rabbits, raccoons, opossums, and fox running all over. I had to know if the deer track I was looking at was a buck or a doe, which way it was heading and whether the tracks were fresh or old. A buck deer huff track is wider at the point than a doe. The point of the huff tells the direction of travel. With all tracks, if the sides are sharp or firm, then the track is fresh, meaning it has been a short period of time since it was made. If the sides of the track are loose and the bottom is rounding, the track is old. However, reading tracks over a period of time, in the same area, can tell you animal habits. Then you can set traps or find a good position to watch the trail.

What you could eat and what not to eat in the woods:

You could eat all of the black and dew berries and Muscadines you could pick and any other fruit trees you could find. Just do not eat too many green plums or apples. That is bad news for the stomach. If you really had to have a BM, you could squat down or bend a small tree over and use it as a seat. You can use moss instead of toilet paper. There were also wild onions you could pick, great with fish, squirrel or rabbit. If you really got hungry, you could always find worms, either under bark of a fallen pine tree or in the ground. They were also good to fish with.

Fishing (with a pole and without a pole):

I forgot to tell you that there was a creek that ran through the 90 acres, it is named Wolf Creek. There were a lot of good deep parts where you could catch perch, trout and cat fish. I first started out using a cane pole with a bobber to let me know when I had a bite. I switch to what they called tight line fishing which you do not use a bobber. You just had to feel the fish pulling on the line.

They also taught me how to use a fishing spear to catch fish at night (gigging). You get some dried pine wood and make a torch with a stick and chicken wire. Then you walk up stream of the creek and spear the fish. Occasionally you will run across a soft shell turtle. That is when you use the 22, it would shoot under water. If you did not have a spear, you could find areas in the creek where you could reach under the bank and feel fish with your hand. I did not like that method. Water moccasin also stayed under the banks. In fact, water moccasins are just in the water period. The last time Daddy, Cousin Tom and I went gigging in the creek together, I was walking between Cousin Tom and Daddy and Cousin Tom said his foot was caught on a root. When he pulled his leg up, it was not a root but a water moccasin. He kicked the water moccasin up on the left bank and I got out on the right bank. Cousin Tom turned around and asks where did I go. That is all it took for me. I made about three steps and was on the bank. I told them "You all catch the fish, throw them up on the bank and I will carry them." They thought that was funny.

Hunting with and without a gun:

Daddy said "Just do not go out there shooting anything that moved, only kill what you are going to eat and do not mess up the meat". What he meant when he said, "Do not mess up the meat" is, shoot rabbits and squirrels in the head. One, they do not run off and two, you do not have to bite down on buck shot when you are eating them. Hunting rabbits in the day time to me was luck. You may run up on one as you walk through the woods and hope it stopped long enough where you could get a good shot. Speaking on walking through the woods, they taught me how to walk on leaves, rocks and twigs and not make any noise. Squirrel hunting was the most fun, because you had to out Fox the squirrel. Whether you were walking or sitting next to a tree, the fun part came when you spotted the squirrel. Squirrels are always going to run for a tree and hide on the side away from you. Pick up a stick and throw it on the side where the squirrel is and it will move around to your side of the tree. Now you have a clear shot, remember head shot. It is even cooler when you have a dog. Once the squirrel is treed, you use the dog the same way you use the stick. Daddy had a Croker sack (a sack made of a course material such as burlap) full of traps. He did not use them a lot, but he did teach me how to implore them. My favorite was setting a trap for a raccoon in the water. Attached foil to the pan on the trap and place it near the bank of the creek about three inches under the water. The raccoon sees the foil and will reach down and try to get it and set off the trap. Snares were the easiest to build; all you needed was some rope and a tree that would bend. Just make sure it is not the tree you used when you had the BM. I also liked quail hunting, except it was not much hunting. Daddy hated to bite down on buck shot. So quail hunting consisted of building a wooden frame approximately five feet long, four feet wide and 18 inches high. Cover it with chicken wire, cut a hole on one side approximately four inches in diameter and four inches from the bottom. Shape a cylinder made out of chicken wire to fit the hole and long enough to reach the middle of the cage. Construct a door on the top where you can reach in. Dig a hole in the ground that the cage will fit in where the hole on the side is level with the ground. Put some corn in the cage. The quail will walk around the cage until they come to the hole, walk down the ramp, drop down into the cage and eat the corn. Once they get full, they can never figure out to come back to the middle of the cage to get out; they keep walking around the sides. Open the door, catch one and pull the head off.

Building a shelter

Building a shelter was the easiest skill I had to learn. The biggest thing is to find a piece of ground that has some trees you can use to attach the floor and roof support to. The floor had to be up off of the ground. I am to scare of snakes to sleep on the ground. I had watched and helped Daddy and a friend of his from Kountze called "Big James" build a room on the back of our house and the camp house, so I understood what I had to do. Just to have something to do and when I found out I had to spend three days in the woods by myself as part of my Rite of Passage, I started building a shelter that was off the ground and had a roof and three sides. It was on the side of a hill that overlooked the pasture. That is the side that I left open. I got smart and took Croker sacks and made me a hammock. I lined the shelter roof with plastic to keep out the rain and cover it with limbs. When I did not have anything to do, I would go and work on it or just enjoy the scenery. I also used it as a hunting stand. Daddy and Cousin Tom told me that I had done a good job, once they found it.

As Daddy and Cousin Tom had done, I had to go out in the woods and stay for three days (Rite of Passage). All I could take was my single shot 22 and 10 rounds, two fishing hooks with five feet of fishing line, a box of matches (Thank God!, I can start a fire with two sticks, but that takes time), a wool army blanket, and my hunting knife. Well, I made it with no problems. Caught some fish and shot a squirrel, picked some wild onions and berries. I started to go over to the pea patch (where all of the crops we growing), but that would have been cheating.

I got back that Monday evening, Daddy and Cousin Tom where at Cousin Tom's house. I came in and they did not say a thing, they each shook my hand and each handed me a handmade ankle bracelet, a sign that I had become a man and past my first test. The second test was to kill a deer. As daddy and Cousin Tom shook my hand, I saw that approval/proud smile on Daddy's face.

Reflective:

I always wanted to make my Daddy proud. I loved the woods, what kid would not love it. Well let me back up, it really depends, I think on genes. For example, my son hates the out of doors and that's cool. My daughter on the other hand, loves the out of doors and is comfortable feeding cows as she is attending a formal event. She shoots just as well as I do, especially with a pistol. Daddy wanted me to have the ability to provide for my family no matter what the circumstances were. Hopefully there is something that your father showed you how to do that you thought was insignificant at the time, but he thought was important. Try and understand why he felt that way.

LITTLE LEAGUE BASEBALL

Like I said, baseball was the only thing that got me out of working at the "barbeque pit". It did not totally get me out of working. I still had to go and help make sausages on Saturday, and I caught the bus home to make a game. The only thing bad about that was I did not get any of the regular money; I had to leave before the lunch crowd came in.

Daddy said to "Play outfield, because all you have to do is run, catch the ball and hit". So, I played the out-field. Beside, my arm was not strong enough to pitch. He showed me how to throw all of the pitches he threw back in the Negro League. It was good to know how to throw them, so I knew how the ball reacts on certain pitches when I was at bat. A curve ball has a black dot in the mid-dle the ball which is made by the laces as it spins. A fast ball had no dot, different spin. Of course a knuckle ball has very little spin.

I started off throwing the ball high in the air, thinking to myself that I was Willie Mays, and catch it, no basket catches. Sometimes, Daddy and I would practice catching and he would throw the ball in the air, so I could work on getting under the ball. My hitting practice consisted of us going over to the park and he would pay some of the kids to shag balls as I hit them. He would tell me which pitch he was going to throw so I could swing according to the pitch. He still had some stuff on the ball although he was just starting in the first phase of Parkinson disease.

WHEN FATHERS DON'T HUG

I started out playing left field, but was switched to center field because of my speed. During the summer, most of our games were at night during the week and on Saturday afternoons, so Daddy got a chance to see me play after he closed up the "barbeque pit".

Remember, I said I had the biggest arms from chopping and splitting wood, well that bat felt like a tooth pick. I think Daddy had me chopping and splitting wood to build up my arms for batting. Right!! He gave me a piece of a broom handle and had me to practice turning my wrist over as you do when you are swing a bat, so I ended up with quick wrist. The result was I ended up batting cleanup, which means I batted fourth in the lineup. For those of you that are baseball challenged, the theory is, the first three batters get on base, and then the fourth batter hits the ball to a part of the field or a home run to "clean" the bases or allow the three base runners to score.

Since Daddy was a pitcher, he worked with our pitchers. We had five, Nathaniel Hawkins; he played football for the Houston Oilers, Kenneth Ellison, Marshall Elo, Paul Mitchell and Patrick Mitchell, no relations to Paul. He taught all of them to throw a knuckle ball and how to mix up their pitches. I think Nathaniel was the best, because he really understood how to work a batter. Kenneth was a little guy and threw very slow. His curve looked like it was falling off of a table and it took forever for his changeup, a pitch that is thrown slower that other pitches, to get to the plate. Marshall could only throw hard and his fast ball was his only pitch. Behind Nathaniel was Paul Mitchell. Daddy taught Paul how to use the corners of the plate. Mr. Billy Williams, our coach, would start Kenneth off pitching with that slow stuff and then bring in Marshall to throw it by them. I saw that approval/proud smile whenever one of the pitchers had a good game. He would always go to them, congratulate them and tell them where they needed to improve.

He would always sit at the top of the bleachers and listen to what folks were saying about my play. He never would talk to any of the people in the bleachers; he said "I do not want folks to know you are my son, so they will be honest in their comments about you". After one of our home games, on the way home, he told me that people were saying that when a ball was hit to center field, that the batter was out, because I had what they called a "good glove". And when I came up to bat, they knew I was going to get a hit. I never knew his physical reaction to what people were saying about me, but I do remember two occasions that that approval/proud smile came out.

The first time was during a game at Emancipation Park, in Houston's Third Ward. I cannot remember what holiday it was, but our game had been advertised with flyers all over Houston and on the local black radio stations. It was a big deal, we were undefeated that year. We were playing an "All Star" team from the Sunnyside part of town. The pitcher, Melvin, for that team was my coach's nephew. We had played him before, so we knew what kind of pitches he threw. I was at bat for the first time in the game, with one man on base. Melvin knew I could hit, so he was trying to work the corners on me. Well, he threw a curve ball that did not break and hit me in the side, all the air left my body. I was trying to shake it off and act like it did not hurt, because there were a lot of pretty girls at the game. I made it to first base, where they tried to get air back in my system. Mama came to the dugout and watched as they loosen my uniform so I could breathe. Daddy never left the stands. Melvin said he was sorry, and that is just baseball. The next time at bat, there were two men on base. Melvin threw a couple of curve balls that had missed the plate. He then threw a fast ball right across the middle of the plate. I made a good swing and hit the ball to left center field. The swimming pool at the park was outside of the field lights on that side of the field. The ball hit in the gap and rolled to the pool fence for a standup double. On the way home, all Daddy said was good hit.

The second time, we were playing a Fourth of July game in the Acres Homes section of town. It was against a team that we had played numerous times. The opposing coach had told my coach that they were going to feed us. Well, we got there and they said they did not have enough food for us. That pissed us off and we ended up going to McDonalds. We all said that they were going to pay for that mistake. The game went on and they were up by one run. It was my time at bat, Anthony Willis was on second and T.J. Williams was on first. Cole, the pitcher for the other team, had thrown a couple of pitches at me to get me from so close to home plate. I loved fast balls, especially one belt high. Well Cole threw one, you guessed it, belt high and across the middle of the plate. At that park, there was a fence that covered left field and part of center field. Behind the fence was a street, with deep ditches on both sides of the street. On the other side of the far ditch was a field that had grown up. Well, I hit the ball over the fence and it landed in the field on the other side of the street for a three run home run. That was the first time I had hit a ball over a fence for a home run. All the other fields we played at did not have fences, so if you could run fast and beat the throw in, you got a home run. Daddy did not see me hit that home run; Mama and Mr. Williams told him about it. His only comment was "You need to learn to hit a curve ball like you hit that fast ball". The next week, I overheard him telling one of his customers about the home run I hit. You could hear that approval/proud smile in his voice.

Daddy got me a tryout my senior year in high school with Charles "Tex" Harrison, besides his basketball career, he was a scout for the Houston Astros. My arm just was not strong enough.

Reflective:

Baseball was Daddy passion, he loved the sport and so did I. What father would not want to see his son make it to the big leagues? He was trying in his own ways to give me some alternates at life. I had learned how to BBQ and I was good at baseball. He gave me all he had to give. Think back on the lessons you learned from your father and reflect on how they have influence your life and your children life.

HUNTING WITH THE BIG BOYS

Daddy would close up the "barbeque pit" at the beginning of deer hunting season and manage hunting camps for different companies. This was usually from the beginning of November to the first of January. Since my mother worked at the "barbeque pit", she had a two month vacation. Before I started school, she and I would catch the bus and go to her home town of Cuero, Texas, southwest Texas, to visit her mother and sister for those two months. When I started school, we would go there during the Christmas breaks. Daddy would come through Cuero and pick us up after he closed down the hunting camp. That gave him a chance to go out to Cousin Sis Williams, who lived outside of Cuero on her farm. He liked to go out there and drink strong coffee with her and hunt squirrels with her son. Daddy would take me hunting with them and it was my job to carry the squirrels they shot. I remember one day we were sitting next to this big oak tree hunting and were not seeing any squirrels, so Daddy and Cousin Floyd decided to walk down by the river and back. Well I had fallen asleep and rather than wake me, they left me by the tree sleep. It was no worries about snakes since it was winter time and I was real warm. Mama had a fit when Cousin Floyd talked too much. After my grandmother passed, we did not go to Cuero that much, so I would catch the bus from Houston to wherever he was.

Daddy was paid fifteen dollars a day. That was okay money for back then, plus he had the best of both worlds. He was getting paid for something he loved to do. He had a budget for all of the supplies and brought anything he wanted or needed. He always came home with a bunch of ammo and other hunting related stuff. The guests that came to hunt were mostly upper level management of companies that did business with the company he was working for. Every hunting site was different as to the number of hunting blinds that he could place hunters in. Daddy would always have two or three hunting blinds where he would place the presidents and vice presidents where there were a high percentage of them killing a buck deer. Most time, this lead to a big tip. He made more in tips in a week than he got paid for the two months.

This particular year, Daddy was managing a hunting lease for Hill & Hill Truck Line, in a place close to Hackberry, Texas. The place was great. There were deer, turkey, wild hogs, squirrels, raccoons, ring tails and coyotes. I could home my tracking and hunting skills.

One of the guest's sons came along with him and was about 20 years old. I was about thirteen or fourteen. He wanted to go squirrel hunting, so Daddy ask me to take him down to this huge pecan grove. There must have been 75 to 100 pecan trees. It was a great place to hunt squirrels. I cannot remember the kid's name, for some reason. Does not matter, I do remember he was carrying a 410 shotgun and I was carrying a 22 lever action Winchester which Daddy had brought me. We put a 2x power scope on it and it held 25 rounds, no reloading after every shot. There were so many squirrels in that pecan grove, you could just walk through the middle and look for them running along the ground or through the trees. We ended up killing five squirrels. When we got back to the lodge, we took our kill into the kitchen, where daddy and the kid's father were talking. We laid them on the table on a piece of paper. Daddy told the kid, graduations on killing those two squirrels. The father asks Daddy how he knew that his son had killed only two squirrels. Daddy said, "The other three are shot in the head". That was his way of an approval/proud smile.

The year previous to the squirrel hunt, I had killed my first deer on that hunting lease. Daddy had found this draw that lead up to a game preserve. He had started feeding this site and only used it for special guest (making sure he got a tip). He called it the fox hole blind. He had dug down about two feet and build the deer blind that looked like a pile of trash. It had a roof on it and the sides had plastic and burlap on the inside to keep out the wind and cold. We also took a little Coleman stove that did not make any noise. It was real toasty in there. He and I hunted that blind the entire time I was there, waiting for a big buck to show up. We had seen a bunch of spike bucks (two points), but no big bucks. It was getting close to the time he was to break camp and he wanted me to kill a buck to fulfill my last Rite of Passage requirement. Just about dusk, what I thought was a three point buck came out into the open. You shoot a deer right above his front shoulder blade, in order to get a heart shot. One, you do not want it to suffer and two; you do not want it to run to far. Ideally, you want it to drop where you shot it. I took aim, pulled the trigger and the deer jumped and ran down the draw toward where we had parked the truck. When we got to the buck, he was dead. Daddy's rule was you shot it you gut it, which was no problem; I had gutted deer that he had killed before. Well, I shot the deer to far back and when the bullet exploded inside him, some of the fragments hit his punch, his guts. Let just say that was a very smelly situation. Daddy told me to finish gutting the deer and he would go and get the truck. I got everything out of the deer that had to come out and threw it over to the side. Daddy, in his humorous mode, can back in the truck and put on brake so that the tires ran right over all of that "stuff" and it went everywhere. Right after I shot the deer and when it dropped he said "you got him!" His other comment was after he ran over that stuff; "you should have shot him better and you would not have to smell that". Once we got back to the lodge, we took pictures and you could see that approval/proud smile.

Reflective:

This experience goes with Learning to Survive. Like I said in the Learning to Survive reflective, hopefully there is something that your father showed you how to do that you thought was insignificant at the time, that he thought was important. Try and understand why he felt that way.

LEARNING TO DRIVE

addy's way of learning something's involved the school of hard knocks. For instant, Daddy and Cousin Tom learn to swim in the creek. It was after their uncles threw them in the creek and it was sink or swim. When Mama heard that, she immediately enrolled me in swimming classes at the park pool. I was not so lucky when it can to learning how to drive.

I cannot remember what age I was when I actually started driving (you notice I did not say driving a car), but I do remember sitting in Daddy's 1948 Chevrolet Pickup truck behind the barbeque pit shifting the truck like I was driving. It came in handy once I started to drive.

Remember "The Camp", family land in east Texas. Daddy and Cousin Tom purchased an old jeep and left it at The Camp. Daddy's idea of learning to drive was take the jeep and drive around the pasture and up on the hill. This gave me a lot of practice shifting and driving up and down a hill. Oh, Daddy and Cousin Tom also said, while you are out there, check the fence line. I had run the fence line (check for breaks in the barb wire fence and fit them) before, but had done it on foot. This meant I had to drive up in the woods between trees. At least I did not have to pack the spool of wire. Daddy's other advice was do not hit any trees, yea right. Along the fence line, the woods were real thick and you could not drive along the line. There was however a trail that ran on both sides of the line which you could walk. I figured out where I needed to park the jeep and hit the trail, trying not to double back.

The next toy Daddy and Cousin Tom purchased was an old red tractor that you had to crank like an old Model T Ford. The gas pedal was a level on the steering column that you pushed forward to increase speed and pull back to decrease speed. It did have brakes. If it was not bad enough that the crank could break your arm trying the start it, you could get thrown off of it if it got away from you. They used it to plow up the field where we grew crops. They also used it to attach to the sugar cane mill when we made syrup. That was the only time I would drive it, actually I would just sit on the seat, did not have to steer. They had the wheels locked so it would go in a circle. That thing was scary, the back wheels were about five feet tall and it was long and make out of cast iron and steel.

I could tell Daddy was afraid of me driving it. This is one time he did not have to worry about me asking to drive that thing. I beat him to the caring this time.

Reflective:

I really did not understand what he was trying to do with this experience until, while we were working for Mr. Ebb, and Daddy said "Learn how to drive a tractor/trailer, make sure you can back in a trailer from both sides". Once again he was trying in his own ways to give me some alternates at life. I could add truck driving to the BBQ and baseball skills. His advice may have come in a statement like, "Don't be like old so and so" or "They ain't going to amount to a hill of beans".

COLLEGE DAYS

I graduated from Booker T. Washington High School in Houston, Texas in May 1968, received a 4 year Army ROTC scholarship and went to Prairie View A&M College in Prairie View, Texas (45 miles northwest of Houston). My freshman year was the last time Daddy managed a deer hunting camp. We had a good time. But it was cold. I mean cold. It was so cold that my fingers stuck to the barrel of my gun and the sky was gray looking. Well, I wanted to go hunting that day and Daddy said it was too cold, but if I wanted to go he would take me out to a blind while he made a trip into town to get some supplies. I had the little Coleman stove that we used to keep warm, but it was not helping. I had so many layers of clothes on I could not lower my arms down by my side. I guess I had been in the blind about an hour when I decided that it was not worth it and would walk back to the camp house along the road. I got down out of the blind and walked approximately an eight of a mile when I saw Daddy coming around a bend. The truck heater was on high and he had a hot cup of coffee for me. When I got in the truck, he had a serious look on his face. All he said was, "Are you ok?"

When we broke camp; he had a lot of can goods and liquor left over. Daddy dropped me off at Prairie View on our way back along with two cases of liquor and a little change in my pocket. Could not let anyone know I had the liquor, you couldn't have any liquor on campus. My roommates and I did not have to buy any liquor for that entire semester.

Daddy and I have some cousins that lived outside of Prairie View and had enough land to hunt on. Daddy would drive over to Prairie View and we would go hunting with Cousin Richard Bean. Do not remember killing anything, but it was like old times, him and I walking through in the woods together. Not making a sound as we walked on leaves and rocks and between bushes. It was great. It was not like when I was learning all of the skills. It was like two hunters going to kill food for the family. I must admit, I found myself watching out for him as he had done for me when I was growing up. You know, when I look back on it, I really did not care if we killed anything or not. It was just great hanging out with him.

I did not know that Daddy loved NASCAR. He would pick me up at Prairie View and drive over to the Texas Motor Speedway right outside of College Station, Texas. We would always stop somewhere and get something to eat and Daddy would get him a six pack of Lone Star Beer. We would watch the race and bet (no money) on who was going to win the race. On the way back to Prairie View, we would go to the Duck Inn in Waller, Texas (five miles from Prairie View). The Duck Inn had the best food, the Chile Cheeseburger and fries with a quart of beer was a meal. He would always give me something for my pocket and tell me not to spend it all in one place.

I took 22 semester hours my last semester at Prairie View. I had to graduate as quickly as I could. The Dean of Men, who was my graduate fraternity brother, had sent a message by way of one of my undergraduate brothers that we were partying too much, especially Jay Dee, Ira, Chester and me. He could never catch us doing anything wrong and we all had GPAs of 3.5 and above. Because I took so many hours that semester, I was finished with classes in December 1971. Prairie View only had graduation in May and August. If you finish all of your requirements in December, you could come back and march in May. Since I and seven other ROTC cadets had fulfilled all of our ROTC requirements, we had a Commissioning Ceremony. Mama cried the whole time and Daddy just sit there. When the ceremony was over, Daddy gave me a real firm handshake and he had the biggest approval/proud smile on his face that I had ever seen.

Reflective:

It was great that Daddy and I could spend some time together while I was in college. It was like making the drive from the packing house to the BBQ pit on those Saturday morning. I was looking at pictures of my commissioning and ran across the picture of him shaking my hand. A lot of emotions surfaced. Find pictures of some special events that you were in that your father attended and see if there are any with him in them. Look at his expression; hopefully you will see a smile.

ARMY DAYS

After commissioning, I married my college sweetheart, Sharon Shipmon, and we headed off to Fort Benning, GA so I could attend the Infantry Officer Basic Course, Airborne school and Ranger school. I accomplished two of three, hurt my back in airborne school and reinjured it during the third week of Ranger School. I was also scheduled to go to Vietnam after Ranger School, but got my orders changed when President Nixon started pulling troops out. You could only go to Vietnam if you had already had a tour there. So my orders were changed to Fort Ord, California.

Daddy and Mama came out to California to visit and I got to show them around the post. Part of Fort Ord was a basic training center and I was the Training Officer for Company C, 3rd Battalion 1st Training Brigade. We went by my company and Daddy though it was so funny to see the trainees pin their self against the wall and yelling "Make a hole, make it big" as we walked down the hall. Mama ask me why were they doing that, and I told her it was for me. As I introduced them to my Company Commander and he began to tell them what an outstanding officer I was, I could see how proud Daddy was of me. You could really see how proud he was of me when he talked to my Drill Sergeants and they told him that I was a soldier's officer, meaning I took care of soldiers first and was hard core. Remember, Daddy served in WWII.

The next time they paid a visit, I was stationed at Fort Hood, Texas. At that time I was the Company Commander of a 140 man air assault company. An air assault company uses helicopter as their mode of transportation. We were getting ready for a pass and review ceremony and were conducting practices. Daddy and Mama came out to the parade field and got a chance to see me commanding my company. When the practice was over, I introduced them to my Battalion Commander. You could see how proud Daddy and Mama were when my Battalion Commander told them that I was one of two lieutenants that were Company Commanders and the two of us were the exceptions rather than the rule.

Reflective:

Daddy did not know it, but he and Cousin Tom had trained me in all the skills I needed to be an infantry officer. Going to the field was like going hunting and shooting weapons was a piece of cake. Try and remember all of those things that your father taught you directly or indirectly, hopefully you can see how they have affected your career and life.

BEING A GRANDPARENT

Sharon got pregnant with our first child, Shere Michelle Kirkwood, while I was stationed at Fort Hood. We had built a home in Houston and Sharon had moved there and was teaching school. Although Sharon is a good cook, as you know it is hard to cook for one person, and since Mama had to cook, Sharon would just go by their house and eat dinner. That suited Sharon and Daddy just fine. Sharon could eat all she wanted and Daddy was going to make sure it was there. On day Mama had cooked a lemon pie and Daddy had set his mouth to eat a piece. Well, Sharon came by to eat as usual, and ate the whole pie. Daddy came into the kitchen and asks Mama, where is the pie. Mama said Sharon ate it. Daddy said the whole thing; Sharon said she thought it was for her. Shere came into this world weighing 8 pounds and 14 ounces. She was born in the morning and Mama and I had been at the hospital all night. After everything was over and Sharon and Shere were ok, I called Daddy and told him about his granddaughter. I told him that I was going home to clean up and he told me to call him once I got cleaned up. When I called him, all he said was "I am ready to go to the hospital". I went by and picked him up, as we walked up to the window, I pointed Shere out. A big smile came over his face and all he said was "She looks like a little papoose". And that was the start of a relationship like I had never seen before. Because Sharon had a C-section, she had to stay in the hospital for a few days and Shere came home with my Mama. Shere only had to make a sound and Daddy was telling Mama to go see about that baby.

Once Sharon went back to work, Shere stayed at Mama and Daddy's house during the day and Sharon would pick her up and eat dinner in the evening on her way home. When it was cold, Sharon would just leave her over there so she did not have to come out in the weather. The first eighteen months of Shere life was spent mostly with her grandparents.

We found out the hard way that Shere could not wear pampers, she broke out in a rash. One day Sharon dropped Shere off and she had a rash from the pampers. When Sharon came to pick her up, Daddy said "Just leave her where she is, she did not have a rash when she left here yesterday". Sharon just turned around and headed for home.

As Shere got older and began to talk, they got even closer. She would get behind him in his chair and rub his bald head or climb up and set in his lap. All she had to say was "Paw Paw, I need that", pointing at a picture in a catalog. He would immediately tell Mama to go to Montgomery Wards and get it. Then I had to put it together.

Shere went to church with Mama every Sunday. When she got ready, she would ask Daddy did she look pretty. He would always tell her "Yes, and be a good girl in church". Daddy loved hot Shipley Donuts and I would stop by the donut shop on my way home and buy two dozen hot glaze donuts! Daddy would wake Shere up at 2:30 in the morning to eat hot donuts. To this day, she cannot pass by Shipley Donuts without stopping.

I had a cousin say that Shere is like the way she is because of me and Mama raising her the way we did and it was difficult for anyone else to break her code. Well, I think they better go back and add in Daddy. She has a lot of his traits which you can still see today.

She got away with stuff that I would have gotten by butt beat for. She was his heart and he was and is still hers.

Reflective:

There is definite difference between the treatment of children and grand children and that is ok. It did not help that his grand child was a girl. Look at your kids and see what traits they have that your father has. It may give you some insight on why they act the way they do.

HIS HUMOROUS SIDE

Daddy had, based on my opinion, a somewhat weird humorous side. All men of his age use the old pull the finger trick. It was a while before I figured out that it did not work, damn near pulled my finger out of the socket.

Daddy made his own hot sauce for the BBQ pit. It was hot. It was hotter than four acres of peppers. I remember one Saturday afternoon while working at the pit, a guy came in drunk. He had been next door at the beer joint. He ordered a link and once I served him, he started covering that link with hot sauce. We usually told customers that it was hot and use it wisely. When I went to tell him about the sauce, Daddy stopped me. I just went and got him another glass of water. Well he ate that link and drunk about five glasses of water. You could see big drops of sweat popping off of his forehead while he was eating. When he left he was sober. Daddy thought that was so funny to see him sweating, blowing and chewing at the same time.

The reason I started down this hot sauce road is I want to tell you his joke about hot sauce. He said he was managing a deer hunt one time and made some deer Chile and put some of his hot sauce in it and put in too much and no one could eat it. So he threw it out over by the trash pile. The next year, Daddy said when he returned to the camp site to set everything up, there were three coyotes waiting for the Chile to cool so they could eat it.

One Saturday morning after we had left the packing house picking up meat, we stopped for a traffic light. Well this guy on a bicycle passed between our truck and the car next to us and went into the intersection and ran right into an oncoming car. The impact knocked him, along with his bike up in the air and him and the bike did a full turn in the air and landed with the bike under him on the hood of the car. The guy was not hurt, but Daddy kept laughing at that full turn he made in the air.

One other day, after we had left the packing house, there was a nun walking down the street. Daddy asks me if I wanted to make five dollars. I said sure, doing what. He said he was going to drive slow and close to the Nun and I was to knock her veil off her head. He kept describing many variations of what she could have said or done.

When I was a little boy, Daddy and Mama took me to Play Land Park. Play Land Park was located on South Main Street and was the precursor to Six Flags over Texas. I do not remember riding but one ride. It was the roller coaster. Well Mama did not want me to ride it by myself, so both of them rode with me. We got in one of the cars and they put me in the middle. The guys locked the bar in place and there was a tug and the cars began rolling and we soon were being pulled up the first hill. That part was cool, but after we got to the top and started down. That was the worst feeling; my stomach felt like it was in my throat. When we started up the second hill, Mama said "Everett!" He said "What!" She said "Hold James!" He said "Hold James, who in the hell gonna hold me". When we finally got off of the roller coaster, Daddy said that was the first time his butt hole had been up around his neck because he could smell it.

He had some saying also, like "It is raining like a double bladder cow pissing on a flat rock"; or "He or she are so black, if they passed gas in a room, they would leave creosote in it", or "you were gone so long, I thought you went to take a crap and the hog caught you", and "He or she are so fat, they look like a bale of cotton with the middle ban missing". If he saw a person wearing some-thing to small, he would say "That is tighter that Dick's hat band". When he saw a person with a big butt, he would say "Their butt is wider than a lot gate". A lot gate is approxi-mately eight feet long. When he got hungry, he would say "I have enough slack in my stomach to make an elephant a mini blouse". There were a number of times we would be riding in the truck and he would be talking. Most of the time I would be listening, sometime I would be thinking about something else. When I would realize that he may be talking to me, I would say "who me" and he would reply in that you dummy tone of voice, "No James, who else do you think I am talking to, who else is in the truck". The one I use a lot is "That is better than a poke in the eye". I use it when someone may say something like "I only got back fifty dollars from the IRS".

For some reason, I always wanted to grow my hair long. Daddy was bald in the top and kept his hair cut short on the sides and it was straight. He would always tell me when he thought I needed a haircut, "Your hair is longer than iron taps on a switch engine". Now you have to remember, when he was working on the railroad, it was the early 1900s and steam locomotives were being used. I tried to look it up, but could never find any information on iron taps on a switch engine. They must have been real long.

Here is one he told me when I was playing little league baseball. We did not have a fence at our park or anything to stop the ball if it was hit over your head in the outfield. One night we were playing and I was playing center field and the batter hit a shot into left center field and it rolled for a while. Daddy said that he thought the number on my back was a stationary side; I had to run so far and long to get the ball.

Here are three that he used when talking to people; when replying to how he was doing, he would say "Fair to middling" or "eating one (meal) and skipping (meal) two" and "If the good Lord is willing and the creek doesn't rise" was his reply to I see you later. "If frogs had wings, he would not bump his butt so much" was his reply to if statements.

His crowning glory was when he and Samuel (Uncle Chuffy) Alexander were talking about when they were playing for the Houston Black Buffalo baseball team. Daddy was driving a nine passenger station wagon one night with Uncle Chuffy in the passenger seat. There were about six or seven other ball players sleep in the remaining seat and their gear. The story is; there was a railroad crossing with a train approaching the crossing. Back then, the light on the front of the train not only shown on the tracks but it also covers a lot of the area on both sides of the tracks. Well, Daddy stop the station wagon far enough from the tracks so that the light from the train just covered the car. Uncle Chuffy started yelling, "You can't make it Kirk" and Daddy started yelling "O yes I can". Everybody in the back woke up and hearing the train whistle and seeing the train light flash through the car. Everybody in the back started jumping out of the car and running. Daddy and Uncle Chuffy were laughing their butts off. Every time Daddy would tell that story, tears would come to his eyes. I wish I could have seen that.

Reflective:

I think I should have been a comedian. I think about a lot of funny things when people are talking, just like Daddy did, like him, I just smile to myself and keep my mouth closed. Think about it, you may be more than a chip off of the same block.

WHEN HE GOT OLD

When I started thinking about writing this book and determining what things to include, I knew I had to include this part of his life, but I am finding that this chapter is going to be the hardest for me to write. I really, really enjoyed writing the other chapters. And that is all I better say about that.

By this time, the Parkinson disease and hard arteries had taken its toll and he was starting to go back to his childhood. And he would also get up at night and walk away from the house. So I moved back home to help Mama. I had purchased a female Weimaraner (dog) and had trained her to hunt squirrels; she was good his Daddy. She stayed in the house and if he got up during the night and tried to leave, the dog would wake me or Mama up. She was smart; she could open the screen door to go in and out by herself.

There was one time during the day he walked away from the house and I found him six blocks from the house sitting at the ice house drinking a Lone Star beer. I walked up and before I could start fussing, he said "Don't say anything". So I just sat down and ordered a beer and called Mama to let her know I found him. One night he got up and left the house and the dog tried to wake me up, with no luck. The dog ended up going with Daddy and when we found him the dog was walking with Daddy and had made Daddy walk on the inside next to the ditch. This kept on and I had to put a key lock on both of the doors. It was very difficult for me to watch him go from a very active person who loved the out of doors to a person who just sat in his recliner and watch the soap operas. Sometimes when he would leave the house, he could not remember leaving. The doctor said it was because of a lack of blood getting to the brain.

One evening before I put the "Everett proof locks" on, he was walking down the back steps and fell. We rushed him to the VA hospital and they determined that he had broken his hip and they operated to replace his hip. Well, he developed an infection and they had to remove his left leg above the knee. Then he went into a coma. I was stationed at the 75th MAC in Houston, which was about three miles from the VA hospital. I would go to the hospital during lunch and after I got off of work. That was really hard. One day I came by and there were two orderlies making their rounds turning patients so they would not get bed sores. These two guys just picked Daddy up and flipped him over like he was a hamburger patty. I walked in the room just in time to see Daddy about a foot in the air. I was in uniform and did not care, I went off. My mouth got lose and the little doctor on station was trying to justify their actions. I told her what she could do and I wanted to speak to the head doctor. About that time, a Colonel walked up and asks what the problem was. I explained what had happen. He took care of the matter and just to check, I would drop in at different times to see that he was treated properly.

The last time I visit with Daddy was May 8, 1979. I got off work as normal and drove to the hospital. When I walked into his room, he was lying there with his eyes open. I said "Daddy you are back". He tried to talk but could not move his lips. All he could do was to bite his lip because he was mad because he could not speak. I told him that I would be right back; I was going to get the nurse. I went to the nurse's station and told the nurse what had happen; she told me that she did not think he had come out of the coma. She went to his room with me and when we got there his eyes were closed and he was not responsive. The nurse still did not believe me. I told the nurse that I was leaving and if and when his status changed for the worst to call me. During that time I was into running, I would run an average of 8 to 10 miles each day during week and 15 to 18 miles on Saturdays. When I got home that evening, I really needed to go for a run. About 5:30 am that next morning on May 9, 1979, I received a call from the VA hospital informing me that Daddy had passed. The first question I asked was why I was not called. I do not even remember what lame ass answer they gave me. That is all I have to say about that. I called the funeral home and went for I long run.

Reflective:

That was one of the worst days of my life. I had told him that I loved him before he fell and broke his hip and I stuck in a hug one day as I was shaking his hands. He did not pull back, all was good. I hope your father is still living, do not wait until it is too late to get things off of your chest or just have a heart to heart. If he is not with you, the best thing I can tell you is "Pray".

MY HOPE FOR YOU

I hope you have enjoyed reading about my relationship with my Dad as much as I have enjoyed writing about it. And most of all, I hope you have remembered some moment or time where you can look back and say "My father did love me and cared about me".

And if your father is still living and you do not have a relationship with him or your relationship is not tight, pick up the phone or better yet, go where he is and start communicating with him.